CONTINENTS

SOUTH AMERICA

by Risa Brown

Content Consultant
Sarah C. Chambers
Associate Professor, Department of History
University of Minnesota

CORE
LIBRARY

Published by ABDO Publishing Company, PO Box 398166, Minneapolis, MN 55439. Copyright © 2014 by Abdo Consulting Group, Inc. International copyrights reserved in all countries. No part of this book may be reproduced in any form without written permission from the publisher. The Core Library™ is a trademark and logo of ABDO Publishing Company.

Printed in the United States of America,
North Mankato, Minnesota
042013
092013

♻ THIS BOOK CONTAINS AT LEAST 10% RECYCLED MATERIALS.

Editor: Blythe Hurley
Series Designer: Becky Daum

Library of Congress Control Number: 2013932002

Cataloging-in-Publication Data
Brown, Risa.
 South America / Risa Brown.
  p. cm. -- (Continents)
ISBN 978-1-61783-934-4 (lib. bdg.)
ISBN 978-1-61783-999-3 (pbk.)
1. South America--Juvenile literature.   I. Title.
918--dc23

                                        2013932002

Photo Credits: Dmitry V. Petrenko/Shutterstock Images, cover, 1; Red Line Editorial, Inc., 4, 18, 26; Dima Gavrysh/AP Images, 6; Dr. Morley Read/ Shutterstock Images, 8; Charles Brewer Carias/AP Images, 10; Agencia Estado/AP Images, 12; Luiz Rocha/Shutterstock Images, 14, 43 (bottom), 45; Shutterstock Images, 17, 19, 20, 24, 33, 42 (top and middle); Willie Davis/Shutterstock Images, 22, 42 (bottom); Norman Chan/Shutterstock Images, 28; Jennifer Stone/Shutterstock Images, 30; Celso Pupo/ Shutterstock Images, 34; Kobby Dagan/Shutterstock Images, 36; Eduardo Rivero/Shutterstock Images, 38; Katarzyna Citko/Shutterstock Images, 41; Marcos Labanca/Agencia de Noticias Gazeta do Povo/Estadao Conteudo/ AP Images, 43 (top); Bartosz Turek/Shutterstock Images, 43 (middle)

CONTENTS

TRINIDAD AND TOBAGO

VENEZUELA

GUYANA

Bogotá

FRENCH GUIANA

COLOMBIA

SURINAME

Galápagos Islands

ECUADOR

PERU

BRAZIL

Lima

BOLIVIA

Rio de Janeiro

Pacific
Ocean

PARAGUAY

CHILE

São Paulo

ARGENTINA

URUGUAY

Atlantic
Ocean

Buenos Aires

N

Falkland Islands

QUICK FACTS ABOUT SOUTH AMERICA

- **Highest point:** Aconcagua, Argentina, 22,835 feet (36,749 km)

- **Area:** 6,884,000 square miles (17,834,658 sq km)

- **Distance north to south:** 4,750 miles (7,644 km)

- **Distance east to west:** 3,200 miles (5,150 km) at the widest point

- **Key industries:** Agriculture, mining, forestry, international trade, manufacturing

- **Population:** 402,177,000

- **Five biggest cities:** São Paulo, Brazil; Rio de Janeiro, Brazil; Bogotá, Colombia; Buenos Aires, Argentina; Lima, Peru

- **Three most common languages:** Spanish, Portuguese, indigenous languages

CHAPTER ONE

WELCOME TO SOUTH AMERICA

The fascinating continent of South America offers visitors much to see. The Andes Mountains run along the entire western edge of the continent. They hide volcanoes and the ruins of ancient civilizations. The Amazon region is a tropical rainforest. It has more unusual plants and animals than any other place in the world. South America's biggest

A local woman stands near a geyser eruption at El Tatio Geyser Field in the Andes Mountains in Chile.

A stream flows through a rainforest high in the Ecuadorian Andes Mountains.

cities combine the architecture of historic Spain or Portugal with modern skyscrapers.

South America is located south of Panama and Central America. It stretches north of the equator and south to the Antarctic. It is surrounded by oceans.

South America has every climate and physical feature. There are glaciers and grasslands. There are tropical rainforests and snow-covered mountains. These features are sometimes quite close to one another. Because of these extreme conditions, many plants and animals live next to each other that would normally be miles apart. For example, penguins live next to tortoises on the Galápagos Islands.

Waterfalls

Among the many spectacular natural features in South America, waterfalls are some of the most notable. Angel Falls in Venezuela is the tallest waterfall in the world. The water there drops 3,212 feet (979 m). Iguaçú Falls is a huge system of 275 waterfalls stretching along a two-mile (3-km) cliff. It sits at the border between Argentina and Brazil.

Who Lives in South America?

There is a rich blend of heritages among South Americans. Indigenous peoples lived on the continent first. Spanish and Portuguese explorers arrived during the early 1500s. Settlers from those countries followed. Those settlers also brought Africans to the continent to work as slaves. During the 1800s and

Venezuela's Angel Falls is the world's tallest waterfall.

1900s, immigrants from other parts of Europe, the Middle East, and Asia began to arrive as well.

For much of South America's history, its people have been separated into a privileged class and a poor class. Now a middle class is also growing.

South Americans tend to have strong family bonds. Most holidays are family times. Celebrations are shared by large, extended family groups. These include grandparents, aunts, uncles, and cousins.

What Makes South America Special?

South America is famous for its celebrations of Carnival. This is

Carnival

Celebrations of Carnival in Rio de Janeiro feature gigantic parades with fabulous costumes. The people of Brazil also celebrate in other ways. These include small neighborhood parades and dances. Brazilian families think about Carnival much as Americans think about Halloween. They celebrate with special costumes and face painting. Brazilians sing songs, go to samba dance classes, march with bands, and decorate with big, beautiful flowers.

Children dressed in costumes enjoy a Carnival party in Petrolina, Brazil.

sometimes called the biggest party in the world. Machu Picchu and other ancient ruins continue to puzzle archaeologists. Many medicines used around the world come from plants found only in the South American rainforest. And in 1859, Charles Darwin changed the world of science with his theory of evolution. He realized that the animals on the Galápagos Islands had slowly evolved to adapt to their surroundings. South America is full of fascinating people, places, nature, and history!

CHAPTER TWO

THE LAND OF SOUTH AMERICA

There are three basic physical areas within South America. They are the rugged Andes Mountains, broad grasslands called the pampas, and tropical rainforests along the banks of the Amazon River.

South America boasts several world-record landforms. The Andes is the longest mountain system on Earth. The Atacama Desert is the driest desert.

The hills around Guanabara Bay offer a stunning view of Rio de Janeiro, Brazil, and the surrounding area.

Parts of it never have rainfall at all. Lake Titicaca is the world's highest lake on which boats can be used. The Amazon region has the world's largest rainforest and the river with the most water.

Amazonia

The Amazon is both a river and a rainforest. This river is so wide and deep that ocean-going ships can use it to travel far inland. It begins in the Andes Mountains in Peru. The river then flows across the continent into the Atlantic Ocean. More than 500 rivers flow into the Amazon. This is what makes the Amazon River so big. Some of these smaller rivers run for more than 1,000 miles (1,609 km) before they even reach the Amazon.

Rain falls frequently in the Amazon River basin. The temperature stays between 65 degrees

The Atacama Desert

The Atacama Desert stretches along the west side of Chile for about 600 miles (966 km). This desert is not hot. Its average daily temperature is around 72 degrees Fahrenheit (22°C).

The Kari Gorge is part of Chile's Atacama Desert.

Fahrenheit (18°C) and 90 degrees Fahrenheit (32°C).
All this water and heat means there is a lot of
humidity.

A few indigenous tribes live in villages in the
Amazon. Very few other people try to live there.

The Andes Mountains

The Andes Mountains follow the coastline of the
Pacific Ocean. They stretch for 4,500 miles (7,242 km)

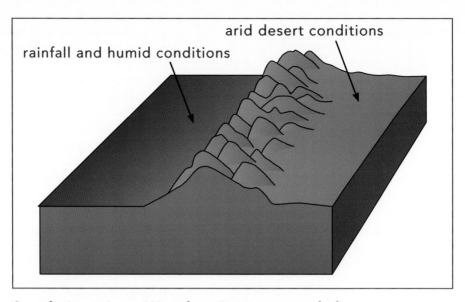

rainfall and humid conditions

arid desert conditions

South American Weather Patterns and the Andes Mountains

The Andes Mountains are responsible for major climate patterns in South America. The mountains are so high that they create a natural barrier that blocks rainfall. In some places this creates lush forests on one side and a desert on the other. So, for example, the Uspalalta Valley in Argentina, which is east of the Andes, is dominated by dry conditions. The Tinguiririca River Valley, which is on the other side of the Andes, is dominated by humid conditions. How do you think these weather patterns might influence the lives of the people in these regions?

and are part of seven different countries. The Andes have both volcanic activity and earthquakes.

People have lived in the Andes for thousands of years. The Inca built cities there, including Machu Picchu. Several large modern cities are also located in these mountains, including Bogotá, Colombia.

The broad, open landscape of the Patagonian pampas in Argentina is ideal for ranching and farming.

The Pampas

As the land flattens away from the Andes to the south and east, it stretches out in broad grasslands called pampas. The soil in this region is fertile and the seasons are very distinct. This makes it ideal for farming. The indigenous people in this region were nomads. This means they moved from place to place and did not have permanent homes.

Cactus trees flourish on the Galapagos Islands.

The Coastlines

South America has thousands of miles of coastline. But there are few places where ships can land easily. Some of South America's largest cities are along the coast. These include Lima, Peru, and Rio de Janeiro, Brazil. Many islands also belong to the countries of South America. The most famous are the Galápagos Islands, which are part of Ecuador.

Gaspar de Carvajal, a Catholic missionary, travelled into the Amazon with Spanish explorers in 1540. He wrote an eyewitness account of his group's encounter with a band of fierce warrior women. The Spaniards called these women Amazons because they were similar to the famous women warriors of Greek mythology:

> *When our approach became known, they [the indigenous people fighting Carvajal's party] went to them to ask for aid, and as many as ten or twelve of those women came. . . . These women were very white and tall, and have very long hair which they wear braided and wrapped around their head, and they are very strong. . . . With their bows and arrows in their hands they fight like ten Indians, and there was one among them who sent an arrow into one of the brigantines a handspan deep, and others less, so our boats looked like porcupines.*

> Source: Gaspar de Carvajal. The Golden Land. *Ed. and trans. Harriet de Onis. New York: Knopf, 1948. Print. 15.*

What's the Big Idea?

Take a close look at Gaspar de Carvajal's words. What is his main idea? What evidence is used to support his point? Come up with a few sentences showing how Carvajal uses two or three pieces of evidence to support his main point.

CHAPTER THREE

SO MANY ANIMALS, SO MANY PLANTS

B ecause of South America's amazing environmental variety, many different kinds of plants and animals live on the continent.

Amazonia

The animals of the Amazon River basin include the capybara, the largest rodent in the world. It is also home to the sloth. The green anaconda also lives in this region. At up to 30 feet (9 m) long, this anaconda

Three-toed sloths live in the rainforests of the Amazon.

Capybaras are as at home in the water as they are on land.

is the longest snake in the world. Piranhas are also found in the Amazon River. Piranhas are fierce fish with sharp teeth and strong jaws that attack anything in the water. One of the most famous Amazonian animals is the poison dart frog. Its skin contains chemicals that can make a person sick.

The tapir is another interesting animal found in the Amazon River basin. These hoglike animals are as large as a pony. The region is also home to jaguars, monkeys, armadillos, giant anteaters, manatees, and river dolphins. There are also more than 500 species of ants. Flocks of parrots, toucans, and macaws fly from tree to tree.

Animals of the Andes and the Pampas

Vicuña and guanaco, which are similar to llamas, live in the Andes Mountains. People have domesticated their cousins, alpacas and llamas. This means they are comfortable working and living with people.

Rubber Trees

The indigenous people of the Amazon River rainforest used sap from rubber trees for many purposes. They made waterproof bags and utensils. They also used rubber to fix leaks in their canoes. When Europeans saw the wonders of rubber, inventors from all over the world began thinking of ways to use it. It was especially important when cars and bicycles, which need rubber tires, were invented. Rubber is still an important industry in South America.

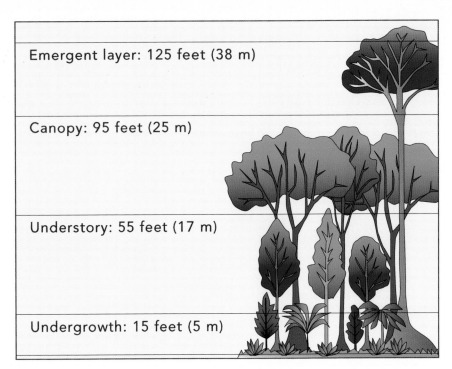

Emergent layer: 125 feet (38 m)

Canopy: 95 feet (25 m)

Understory: 55 feet (17 m)

Undergrowth: 15 feet (5 m)

The Layers of the Rainforest

Dead plants decompose on the rainforest floor because it is dark and humid there. Above the rainforest floor is the undergrowth layer. This is made up mostly of ferns and small bushes. Next comes the understory layer. It is composed of thin trees. Above that, the canopy layer is home to taller trees that almost connect with one another to form a kind of roof. The final layer, called the emergent layer, is a group of trees that punches through the canopy. Imagine yourself climbing a tall tree in the rainforest. As you go up, what differences do you feel in temperature? How bright or dark is it? What plants and animals do you see?

Alpacas grow wool that makes very soft yarn. Llamas are so strong they can carry as much as 130 pounds (58 kg). Rheas, which look like ostriches, also live on the pampas.

Animals of the Galápagos Islands

The Galápagos Islands are close to the equator. But their climate is not tropical. This is because cold ocean currents swirl around the islands. The plants and animals that live there have adapted to these unique conditions. Most of them do not live anywhere else in the world. The Galápagos has its own sea lions, booby birds (some with bright blue feet), penguins, and ocean-swimming iguanas. The tortoises there can grow up to 500 pounds (226 kg).

Many different types of plants grow on the Galápagos Islands. This is because of the different climates found there. In some areas, only cacti and small shrubs can take

Penguins in South America

On a continent that has llamas and sloths, it may be a surprise that South America is also home to penguins. In fact, five species of penguins live only in the southern tip of South America and on the Falkland Islands. These are the King, Gentoo, Southern Rockhopper, Macaroni, and Magellanic penguins.

The seeds of the cacao tree are used to make cocoa powder and chocolate.

hold in the lava-filled soil. But some of the mountains on the islands receive an almost constant mist of rain. This creates the perfect environment for ferns, vines, and rainforest trees and plants.

South American Plants

South America is home to many unusual species of plants. The Amazon River basin has so many plant species that it is sometimes called "the green ocean." The many kinds of trees there support a variety of plant and animal life. Some plants grow on tree trunks. Their roots can take water right out of the air! The orchids found here produce beautiful flowers. Cocoa, vanilla, and several kinds of nuts all come from the rainforest. And the trees of the Amazon produce a large part of the world's oxygen.

CHAPTER FOUR

WHO LIVES IN SOUTH AMERICA?

Just as South America has three basic geographic areas, the people there have developed into three general groups.

The People of the Andes

When Spanish explorers came to the western shore of South America, they found the well-organized Incan society. The Incan people were farmers. They grew crops on terraces and used complex watering

These Peruvian children are dressed in traditional Andean clothing.

Machu Picchu

Machu Picchu is one of the great mysteries of South America. Sometimes called the "city in the clouds," it was built around 1450. Its location on the eastern side of the Andes Mountains kept it hidden from the Spanish conquerors. The Incan people left Machu Picchu right around the time of the Spanish invasion. No one knows why. Machu Picchu was unknown to the outside world until American historian Hiram Bingham discovered it in 1911. Bingham was helped by a local boy, Pablito Álvarez, who was only 11 years old. Since then, Machu Picchu has become an important tourist attraction.

systems. They were also artists who left behind beautiful ceramics and cloth. These people's buildings showed their incredible skill with stonework. How they moved huge granite blocks and fit them together is still a mystery.

The Spanish invaders who came to South America beginning in the 1500s conquered the Inca. These explorers and soldiers did not understand the languages or cultures of the native people. They did not acknowledge that the

The Incan city of Machu Picchu is known for its beautiful stonework and terraces.

land already belonged to the Inca. The Spaniards enslaved many Incan people and their descendants. This persecution of the indigenous people of the Andes continued for hundreds of years.

Today, the combination of native and Spanish cultures can be seen in the music, food, and festivals

A samba school parade marches through Rio de Janeiro, Brazil. Dancing schools and clubs practice all year to prepare for performing at Carnival.

of this area. Feast days celebrate native traditions, such as the Festival of the Sun. Religious festivals include holidays honoring local patron saints. The music of the region often combines folk instruments, such as panpipes, with instruments from Spain, such as harps and guitars.

People of the Tropical Plateau

Portuguese colonists established sugar plantations along the coasts of the tropical plateau during the 1500s. Then gold and emeralds were discovered inland during the 1700s. Mines were established. Colonists brought slaves from Africa to serve as the main source of labor on their plantations and in their mines. Eventually these slaves won their freedom.

African customs and traditions blended with those of the Europeans. Brazilian music was heavily influenced by African music. This resulted in musical styles such as samba, *marchina*, and bossa nova. Many recipes from this area use African spices. Celebrations honor both the African love of nature and the Catholic religious traditions of Europe.

People of the Pampas

The pampas have the least amount of native or African influence in South America. Spaniards brought horses and cattle to this area during the 1800s. Those animals formed large, wild herds. Gauchos, or South American cowboys, earned their living by taming horses and selling cattle hides. These gauchos came from African, indigenous, and Spanish ancestors.

A participant in the annual Patria Gaucha festival in Tacuarembo, Uruguay

During the 1870s, the government of Argentina forced the indigenous people of the pampas to leave their homeland to make way for ranching and farming. Immigrants from all over Europe came to the pampas. As farms became more common, the gaucho tradition died out. But beef is still a big part of the diet in this area.

The people of the pampas share a melting pot of European cultures, food, music, and celebrations that is different from the rest of South America. The best-known music and dance style of the area is the tango.

Pachacutec Inca Yupanqui, who is considered by many to have been the greatest Incan emperor, wrote many hymns between about 1440 and 1450. They are among the world's great sacred poetry. This example celebrates Wiracocha, the creator of the world:

My Wiracocha [the Creator]

shine on your Incan people

illuminate your servants

whom you have shepherded,

let them live

happy and blessed

free of sickness, free of pain.

Source: Yupanqui. Trans. John Curl. "Prayer to the Sun."
The Sacred Hymns of Pachacutec: Ancient Inca Poetry. *John Curl, 2005.*
Web. Accessed December 10, 2012.

Consider Your Audience

Read Yupanqui's poem closely. How could you adapt it for a different audience, such as your parents or younger friends? Write a blog post sharing these same ideas for the new audience. What is the best way to get your point across to this audience?

CHAPTER FIVE

SOUTH AMERICA TODAY

South America is made up of several separate countries. Each has its own government. People throughout South America are now able to vote in order to choose their elected officials. The people and their elected representatives hold the power. However, governments have changed frequently over the years in South America. This has sometimes made it difficult for businesses to grow.

The National Congress in Buenos Aires, Argentina, is home to the legislative branch of the Argentinian government.

Today many new industries are growing in South America. These include computer manufacturing and other technological fields. South America is rich in natural resources such as oil, minerals, and lumber. Businesses have often harmed the environment when they accessed these resources.

The Rainforest

People have burned large sections of the Amazon rainforest to clear the land. They have also cut down many trees for lumber. This destroys the homes of thousands of plants and animals. It also affects the air we breathe. The trees in the rainforest turn carbon dioxide into oxygen. The destruction of the rainforest could lessen the amount of oxygen people have to breathe. Environmental groups around the world are fighting to save the Amazon's rainforests.

Social Change

As South America continues to grow, life is changing for many people. Cities are growing more quickly as people move from the countryside to try to find jobs. Many jobs now require more education. This means people are learning new skills. More South Americans are

Fans support the Boca Juniors fútbol team in Buenos Aires. South Americans show their national pride by supporting their fútbol, or soccer, teams.

getting an education than ever before. South America has a growing middle class of professionals.

South America has problems to face in the future. These include protecting its environment and improving the lives of its less-fortunate people. But many people all over the world think of this special continent as a wonderful place to live, work, and vacation. From its many climates to its wonderful wildlife, South America is truly a place like no other!

Cacti on the Galápagos Islands

The Galápagos Islands

A visit to the Galápagos Islands is a chance to see plants and animals that live nowhere else in the world.

Machu Picchu

Machu Picchu is famous for its amazing stonework and breathtaking views of the surrounding Andes Mountains.

Machu Picchu

The Amazon

Many parts of the Amazon region are just as wild, dangerous, and fascinating as they were before the area's discovery by Europeans.

A sloth in the Amazonian jungle

Iguaçú Falls

Iguaçú Falls

Iguaçú Falls is actually 275 separate waterfalls. Because the water crashes more than 260 feet (79 m), the roar it makes is quite loud.

Lake Titicaca

Lake Titicaca

The Aymara people who live on the shores of Lake Titicaca have kept many of their ancient traditions alive.

Rio de Janeiro

The most famous city in South America, Rio de Janeiro, is surrounded by mountains, ocean, and white sand beaches and is located on the best natural harbor in the continent.

Rio de Janeiro

STOP AND THINK

Why Do I Care?

People in South America live far away from you. Can you find similarities between your life and the lives of kids who live in South America? If you met someone from South America, what would you talk about? Write an e-mail to an imaginary South American pen pal.

Take a Stand

This book discusses how the rainforest provides oxygen for the air we breathe. Do you think the destruction of the rainforest is a problem? Or do people have a right to cut down trees for human uses, such as building houses and making paper? Write a short essay explaining your opinion. Make sure to give reasons for your opinion, and include facts and details that support those reasons.

You Are There

This book discusses explorers who were amazed by the beauty and wonder of South America. Imagine you are a boy or girl leaving your European home to come to South America. Is your new life difficult? How do you describe your new home to your old friends who do not know anything about it?

Say What?

Learning about a different country often means hearing words in a different language. Find five words in this book that are Spanish or Portuguese. Write an English definition of these words and use each word in a new sentence.

GLOSSARY

ancestors
the people from whom someone is descended

archaeologist
a scientist who studies peoples of the past

decompose
to decay or become rotten

economy
a system of making products and selling or buying them

equator
an imaginary line around the center of the earth where the hottest climates are usually found

immigrant
a person who leaves one country to live in another

indigenous
originating or occurring naturally in a particular place

nomad
a person who moves from place to place and does not have a permanent home

persecution
to subject someone to hostility and ill-treatment, especially because of their race or political or religious beliefs

plantation
a large farm

plateau
a broad, flat area of high land

terrace
a way to grow plants on a hill by making a series of flat steps